David has been at his friend's house.

Now he is walking home.

It's dark, really dark!

He takes a shortcut down an alleyway.
There are no street lamps.
A dog jumps out and barks at him.

Get away!
SPLIT

Trouble!
POUCE

He gets to the main road.
A police car has stopped near
some boys. What's up?

He walks under the railway bridge.
There are echoes and strange
noises everywhere.
What was that?

David goes down a quiet street.
There is a noise behind him and
he turns round.
A black cat is following him
in the shadows.
He starts to walk faster.

Go home!

He gets to the underpass.

This is the worst bit.

He doesn't hang around.

Go! Go! Go!

Nearly there...

He has got to the flats where he lives.
The outside light isn't working.
Someone comes out and makes
him jump.

He runs up one floor,
two floors,
three floors,
four floors...
11

He's made it!
He calls out, "Hi, Mum! I'm home!"
He says it as cool as he can,
but he is well scared!